DATE DUE			

30611

599.53
WEL

Welsbacher, Anne.

Killer whales

CENTRAL MIDDLE SC MEDIA CENTER

Predators in the Wild

Killer Whales

by Anne Welsbacher

Scientific Consultant:
Jody Byrum
Science Writer
SeaWorld, San Diego

CAPSTONE
HIGH-INTEREST
BOOKS

an imprint of Capstone Press
Mankato, Minnesota

Capstone High-Interest Books are published by Capstone Press
151 Good Counsel Drive, P.O. Box 669, Mankato, Minnesota 56002
http://www.capstone-press.com

Library of Congress Cataloging-in-Publication Data
Welsbacher, Anne, 1955–
    Killer whales/by Anne Welsbacher.
    p. cm.—(Predators in the wild)
    Includes bibliographical references and index (p. 32).
    Summary: Describes killer whales, their habits, where they live, their
hunting methods, and how they exist in the world of people.
    ISBN-13: 978-0-7368-1065-4 (hardcover)
    ISBN-10: 0-7368-1065-X (hardcover)
    1. Killer whale—Juvenile literature. [1. Killer whale. 2. Whales.] I. Title.
II. Series.
QL737.C432 .W45 2002
599.53'6—dc21   2001002927

Editorial Credits
Blake Hoena, editor; Karen Risch, product planning editor; Timothy Halldin,
    cover designer and illustrator; Katy Kudela, photo researcher

Photo Credits
Beth Davidow/Visuals Unlimited, 16
Betty Sederquist/Visuals Unlimited, 15
Chris Huss/Innerspace Visions, cover
Eda Rogers, 6, 8, 17 (top right)
Gerald & Buff Corsic/Visuals Unlimited, 17 (bottom left)
Hiroya Minakuchi/Innerspace Visions, 22
Ingrid Visser/Innerspace Visions, 12, 20, 21, 29
Jasmine Rossi/Innerspace Visions, 18
Jeff Footi/TOM STACK & ASSOCIATES, 10
Joe McDonald, 17 (top left), 24
Michael S. Nolan/TOM STACK & ASSOCIATES, 14
Mike Nolan/ Innerspace Visions, 28
Robin Brandt, 11, 17 (bottom right)
Thomas Kitchen/TOM STACK & ASSOCIATES, 9
Tom Walker/Visuals Unlimited, 27

1 2 3 4 5 6 07 06 05 04 03 02

Table of Contents

Features

Fast Facts

Common names:	Killer whale, orca
Scientific name:	*Orcinus orca*
Length:	Most killer whales grow to be 16 to 22 feet (4.9 to 6.7 meters) long. Males usually are larger than females.
Weight:	Most killer whales weigh between 3,000 and 12,000 pounds (1,400 and 5,400 kilograms).
Appearance:	Killer whales have a black back and a white underside. They also have a white patch behind each eye.
Life span:	Killer whales usually live 25 to 35 years.

Range:	Killer whales live in all of the world's oceans. But most are found in polar regions.
Prey:	Killer whales eat fish, squid, seals, sharks, sea lions, turtles, birds, and other whales.
Eating habits:	Killer whales eat as much as 100 to 500 pounds (45 to 230 kilograms) of food per day.
Swimming habits:	Killer whales are fast swimmers. They can swim up to 30 miles (48 kilometers) per hour. Killer whales also breach and spyhop.
Social habits:	Killer whales are social animals. They gather in pods. These groups live and hunt together.

In This Chapter:

* Killer whales belong to the dolphin family.

* Killer whales live in groups called pods.

* Killer whales communicate through sounds.

Chapter 1

Killer Whales

Killer whales are one of the largest predators in the world. Predators hunt other animals for food. Most killer whales grow to be 16 to 22 feet (4.9 to 6.7 meters) long. They usually weigh between 3,000 and 12,000 pounds (1,400 and 5,400 kilograms). Male killer whales grow to be larger than females.

   One of the largest killer whales recorded was 32 feet (9.8 meters) long. This whale weighed about 22,000 pounds (10,000 kilograms).

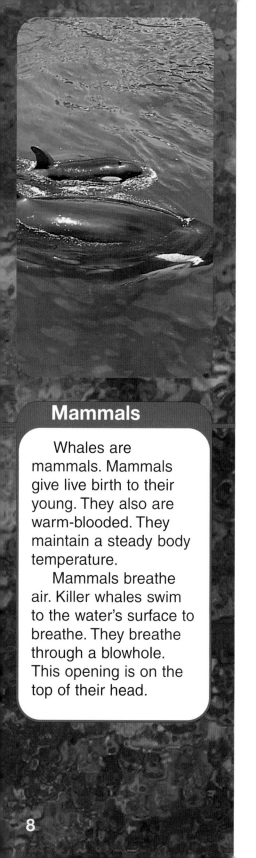

Mammals

Whales are mammals. Mammals give live birth to their young. They also are warm-blooded. They maintain a steady body temperature.

Mammals breathe air. Killer whales swim to the water's surface to breathe. They breathe through a blowhole. This opening is on the top of their head.

Whale Species

Two types of whales exist. Baleen whales include blue whales and gray whales. These whales have thin plates called baleen instead of teeth. Spaces between the baleen allow water to escape as the whales close their mouths. But the baleen traps the whales' food. Toothed whales include killer whales and sperm whales.

Scientists divide whales into families. Killer whales belong to the dolphin family. Killer whales actually are a type of dolphin. But people call them whales because of their large size.

Appearances

A killer whale has a black back and a white underside. It has a white spot behind each eye.

Female killer whales have short, curved dorsal fins.

A killer whale has a thick body and a round head. It has large flippers on its sides. Its tail is divided into two lobes called flukes. A killer whale also has a dorsal fin on its back. A male's dorsal fin stands straight up and may be 6 feet (1.8 meter) tall. A female's dorsal fin is smaller and curved.

Killer whales live in pods.

Life in the Water

Killer whales mostly swim near the surface of the water. They often find prey near the water's surface. But killer whales can dive as deep as 200 feet (61 meters). They can stay underwater for as long as 10 minutes.

Killer whales are fast swimmers. They can swim up to 30 miles (48 kilometers) an hour.

Killer whales may breach. They leap out of the water and land on their back, sides, or underside. This action creates a loud splash. Scientists do not know why killer whales breach. They believe it may be for hunting or communication reasons.

Pods

Killer whales are social animals. They live in groups called pods. Pods usually have 5 to 30 members. Pod members hunt and care for the pod's young together.

Pods sometimes join together. They then form "superpods." Superpods can have more than 100 members.

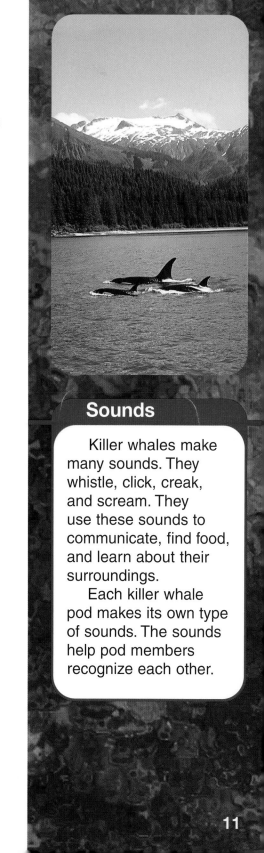

Sounds

Killer whales make many sounds. They whistle, click, creak, and scream. They use these sounds to communicate, find food, and learn about their surroundings.

Each killer whale pod makes its own type of sounds. The sounds help pod members recognize each other.

In This Chapter:

* Killer whales can be resident or transient.

* Killer whales use echolocation.

* Killer whales hunt together to catch prey.

Chapter 2

The Hunt

Killer whales live and hunt in all of the world's oceans. Some killer whales travel from one area to another. These killer whales are called transient. They follow the movements of their prey. Other killer whales live in one area. These killer whales are called resident.

Resident and transient killer whales eat different types of prey. Resident killer whales most often eat fish such as salmon and tuna. Transient killer whales hunt for seals, sea lions, and other whales. Some killer whales have even attacked moose and caribou that crossed the mouth of a river.

Killer whales sometimes spyhop to see their surroundings.

Killer Whale Senses

Killer whales have good eyesight. They can see well under and above water. Their eyesight helps them locate nearby prey.

Killer whales sometimes spyhop. To spyhop, they lift the front half of their body out of the water. This action allows them to see above the water.

Killer whales have an excellent sense of hearing. They can hear high-pitched sounds that humans cannot hear. Killer whales often use high-pitched sounds to communicate.

Killer whales use echolocation to hunt and find their way underwater. Killer whales make clicking sounds. These sounds echo off underwater objects and animals. Killer whales listen to the echoes. They are able to tell an object's size, shape, speed, and distance through echolocation.

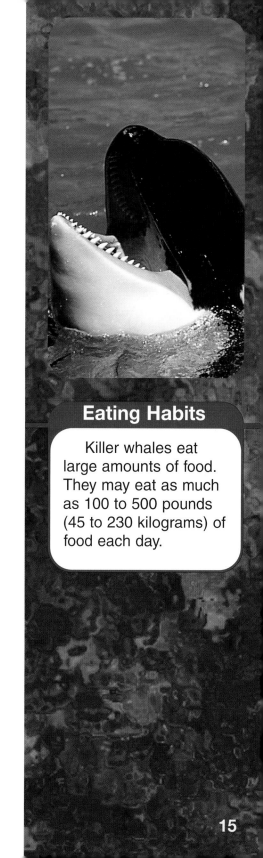

Eating Habits

Killer whales eat large amounts of food. They may eat as much as 100 to 500 pounds (45 to 230 kilograms) of food each day.

Killer whales hunt in groups.

Wolves of the Sea

Some people call killer whales "wolves of the sea." Both wolves and killer whales hunt in groups.

Killer whales work together to catch prey. One killer whale may tip a sheet of ice that a seal is on. Another killer whale then catches the seal when it slides off the ice.

Killer whale pod members often circle around prey such as fish. They do this to herd the fish together. It is easier for killer whales to catch fish that are closely grouped together.

Killer whales also circle around large prey such as other whales. This action prevents the prey from escaping. Killer whales then take turns attacking their prey.

What Killer Whales Eat

Porpoises

Fish

Penguins

Seals

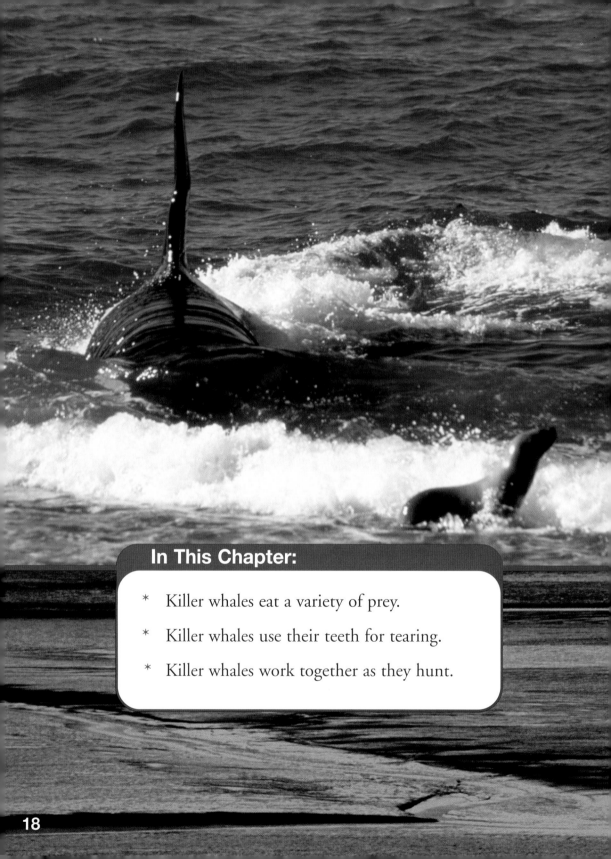

In This Chapter:

* Killer whales eat a variety of prey.

* Killer whales use their teeth for tearing.

* Killer whales work together as they hunt.

Chapter 3

The Kill

Killer whales eat a wide variety of prey. They eat fish, squid, sharks, turtles, and birds. Killer whales are the largest predator of mammals. They may eat seals, sea lions, and other whales.

Killer whales are small compared to many other whales. For example, blue whales may grow to be 90 feet (27 meters) long. But killer whale pods have been known to attack these large animals.

Killer whales sometimes eat even when they are not hungry. They often eat until they are overly full when prey is plentiful. This action allows their bodies to store fat. Extra fat helps killer whales survive when they cannot find as much food. Killer whales spend about half of their time searching for prey.

Teeth

Killer whales have from 40 to 56 sharp, cone-shaped teeth. These teeth are 3 inches (7.6 centimeters) long. They are about 1 inch (2.5 centimeters) thick at the base.

Killer whales' teeth curve toward the back of the mouth. This shape helps them hold onto prey once they catch an animal.

Killer whales do not chew their food. Their long, pointed teeth are good for tearing instead of chewing. Killer whales swallow their food in large chunks. Killer whales can even swallow fish and young seals whole.

Killer whales have long, pointed teeth.

Killer whales sometimes swim onto shore to catch seals.

Attacking Prey

Killer whales surround large prey. They lunge at it from all directions. They bite large chunks of flesh from the animal. This action weakens the animal. Killer whales also may force prey underwater until it drowns.

Killer whales attack smaller prey in several ways. They may herd fish together. A killer whale may leap onto a sheet of ice to push a seal or penguin off the ice. A killer whale sometimes hits a seal with its tail to knock it out.

Some killer whales even slide up onto beaches to catch prey. A killer whale chooses a seal to attack. It then lunges out of the water and onto the beach. It grabs the seal and wiggles back into the water.

Myth versus Fact

Myth: People think killer whales are dangerous because of their name.

Fact: People have been attacked by killer whales. But scientists believe these attacks were made by mistake. The killer whales may have mistaken people for prey. The name "killer whale" actually comes from Spanish whale hunters in the 1700s. They called killer whales "killers of whales."

Myth: Killer whales are fish.

Fact: Killer whales are mammals. Mammals breathe air. Killer whales must swim to the water's surface to breathe. They breathe through a blowhole.

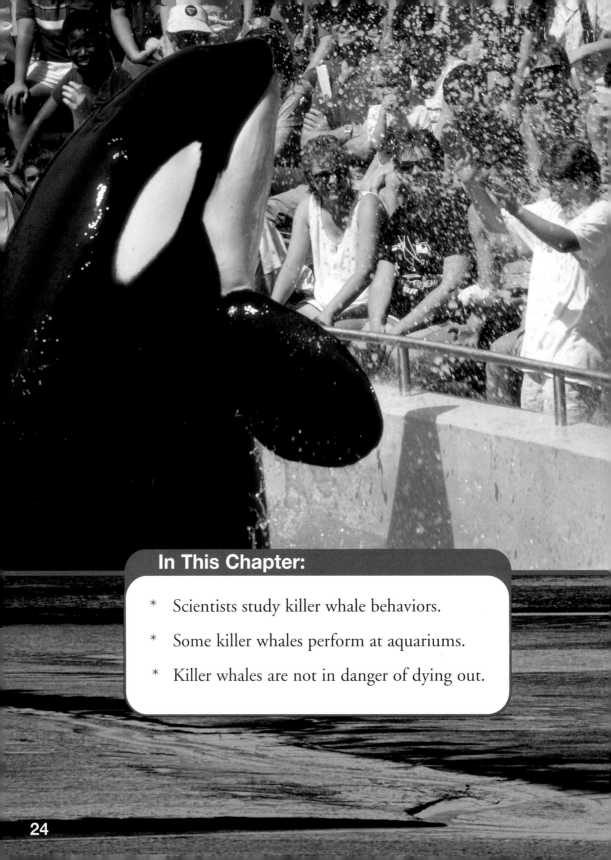

In This Chapter:

* Scientists study killer whale behaviors.

* Some killer whales perform at aquariums.

* Killer whales are not in danger of dying out.

In the World of People

Killer whales live in all of the world's oceans. But most live in polar regions. These areas are near the North or South poles.

Three killer whale pods live in the Pacific Ocean near Vancouver, Canada. These pods include more than 80 whales. Scientists study these killer whale pods. They photograph killer whales' dorsal fins. These photos help scientists identify each whale. They then can follow a certain killer whale throughout its life.

Scientists have learned much about killer whales from these studies. They have watched how killer whales hunt, kill, and behave in their pods.

Killer Whales in Zoos

Some killer whales live in zoos and aquariums.
Trainers train these whales to perform for zoo
visitors. Killer whales play with the trainers who
work with them. They swim with trainers
without hurting them. They even let trainers
put their hands inside their mouths.

Some scientists think that captive killer
whales in zoos are unhappy. Once, captive killer
whales were taken from their pods. But today,
most captive killer whales are born in zoos or
aquariums. The other killer whales at these
places then form the newborn's pod.

Other scientists believe zoos help killer whales. Scientists can easily study and learn more about killer whales in zoos. They then can teach people how to avoid hurting killer whales.

Whale Hunting

Throughout history, people have hunted whales. People used whale meat for food. They also used whale oil to make soaps, perfume, and fuel. Many types of whales have come close to dying out because of overhunting.

People also hunted killer whales. People mostly killed killer whales out of fear. People used to believe that killer whales attacked people on purpose. Today, people do not believe that this is true.

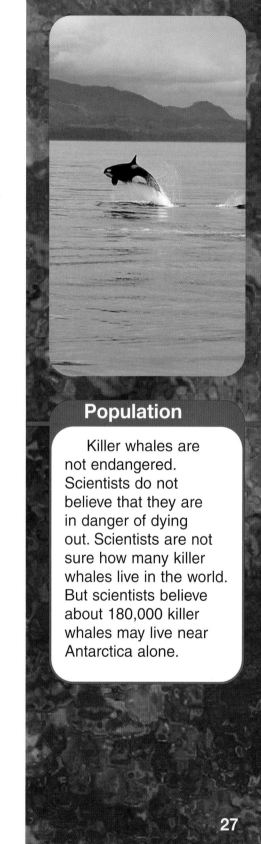

Population

Killer whales are not endangered. Scientists do not believe that they are in danger of dying out. Scientists are not sure how many killer whales live in the world. But scientists believe about 180,000 killer whales may live near Antarctica alone.

Boat Tours

Many people take boat tours to learn more about whales. But scientists worry that whale watching might harm killer whales. Boats may block killer whales from hunting. Boat engine noise might interrupt sounds killer whales make. The noise may scare away prey. Boat propellers sometimes injure killer whales.

Dangers to Killer Whales

Today, people no longer hunt killer whales. But they can harm killer whales in other ways.

Chemicals people use can pollute the ground, water, and plants. Small animals take in tiny bits of these chemicals when they eat. Larger animals eat the smaller animals. The chemicals then build up in the larger animals' bodies. These chemicals eventually can poison larger animals such as killer whales.

Scientists fear that killer whales may be dying at a faster rate than in the past. A decrease in prey in some areas is lowering killer whale populations.

The U.S. government has passed laws to protect killer whales. These laws protect

Killer whales are protected near U.S. coasts.

killer whales near U.S. shores. The U.S. Marine
Mammal Protection Act makes it illegal to harm
or kill killer whales. This law also protects
animals such as sea otters, walruses, and polar
bears. Research and laws help to make sure that
killer whales will continue to survive in the wild.

echolocation (eh-koh-loh-KAY-shuhn)—the process of using sounds and echoes to locate objects; killer whales use echolocation to hunt and to find their way underwater.

fluke (FLOOK)—a part of a whale's tail

habitat (HAB-uh-tat)—the place and natural conditions in which plants and animals live

pod (POD)—a group of killer whales; pods often are made of family members.

predator (PRED-uh-tur)—an animal that hunts other animals for food

resident (REZ-uh-duhnt)—an animal that lives in one particular place

social (SOH-shuhl)—living in groups or pods; killer whales are social animals.

transient (TRAN-zee-uhnt)—an animal that moves from place to place

To Learn More

Bair, Diane, and Pamela Wright. *Whale Watching.* Wildlife Watching. Mankato, Minn.: Capstone Books, 2000.

Carwardine, Mark. *Killer Whale: Habitats, Life Cycles, Food Chains, Threats.* Natural World. Austin, Texas: Raintree Steck-Vaughn, 2000.

Gowell, Elizabeth Tayntor. *Whales and Dolphins: What They Have in Common.* Animals in Order. New York: Franklin Watts, 2000.

Woog, Adam. *Killer Whales.* Nature's Predators. San Diego: Kidhaven Press, 2002.

Useful Addresses

The Marine Mammal Center
Marin Headlands
1065 Fort Cronkhite
Sausalito, CA 94965

SeaWorld San Diego
500 SeaWorld Drive
San Diego, CA 92109-7904

Vancouver Aquarium
P.O. Box 3232
Vancouver, BC V6B 3X8
Canada

The Whale Museum
62 First Street North
P.O. Box 945
Friday Harbor, WA 98250

Internet Sites

Enchanted Learning—All About Whales

http://www.enchantedlearning.com/subjects/
whales

SeaWorld—Killer Whales

http://www.seaworld.org/infobooks/Killer
Whale/home.html

Vancouver Aquarium

http://www.vanaqua.org

Index